The Thirty-Nine Steps

John Buchan

Abridged and simplified by
George F. Wear

and revised by
A. G. Eyre

LONGMAN

LONGMAN GROUP LIMITED
London

*Associated companies, branches and representatives
throughout the world*

First published 1938
Second edition (reset and re-illustrated) 1960
Third edition 1978

ISBN 0 582 52798 8

The publishers are indebted to Messrs William
Blackwood & Sons Ltd. for permission to issue
this simplified and abridged edition.

Printed in Great Britain by
Hazell Watson & Viney Ltd, Aylesbury

Contents

Longman Simplified English Series

This book has been specially prepared to make enjoyable reading for people to whom English is a second or a foreign language. An English writer never thinks of avoiding unusual words, so that the learner, trying to read the book in its original form, had to turn frequently to the dictionary and so loses much of the pleasure that the book ought to give.

This series is planned for such readers. There are very few words used which are outside the learner's vocabulary.[1] These few extra words are needed for the story and are explained in the glossary. Long sentences and difficult sentence patterns have been simplified. The resulting language is good and useful English, and the simplified book keeps much of the charm and flavour of the original.

At a rather more difficult level there is *The Bridge Series*, which helps the reader to cross the gap between the limited vocabulary and structures of the *Simplified English Series* and full English.

It is the aim of these two series to enable thousands of readers to enjoy without great difficulty some of the best books written in the English language, and in doing so, to equip themselves in the pleasantest possible way, to understand and appreciate any work written in English.

John Buchan was born in Scotland in 1875. He went to two universities, first Glasgow and then Oxford, where he gained

---

[1] The 2,000 root words of the *General Service List of English Words* of the *Interim Report on Vocabulary Selection*, and words formed from them, together with about 150 words whose frequency seems to have increased since that list was made.

Introduction and note on the author

the Newdigate Prize for poetry. His life after that was a busy one. After three years as private secretary to Lord Milner in South Africa, he returned to England and worked hard in the field of book production. He was an officer in the First World War, and Director of Information from 1917. In 1927 he became a Member of Parliament, and in 1935, as Lord Tweedsmuir, he went as Governor-General to Canada. All this time he was writing as well. His knowledge of history and his work in the public service brought him respect for his serious works on the lives of great men such as *Oliver Cromwell* (1934) and the record of his own life, *Memory Hold the Door* (1940 – the year in which he died). An even greater public enjoyed his stories of mystery and adventure which included *The Thirty-Nine Steps, Greenmantle, Mr Standfast, Huntingtower, The Three Hostages, The Dancing Floor* and *The Power House* among many others.

The Thirty-Nine Steps is a story of exciting adventures, narrow escapes and the last-minute solution of a deep mystery. It was written in 1915, during the First World War. There is a band of dangerous enemy agents in England. They have killed one man who had discovered something about their plans. Can Hannay find out what that was before they can kill him too?

1. The man who died

I returned from the City about three o'clock on that May afternoon feeling disgusted with life. I had been three months in England and was tired of it. If anyone had told me a year ago that I would have been feeling like that, I should have laughed at him; but there was the fact. The weather made me ill, I couldn't get enough exercise, and the amusements of London did not interest me. 'Richard Hannay,' I kept telling myself, 'this is not the right place for you, my friend. You had better get out.'

It annoyed me to think of the plans I had been building up in the last few years in Bulawayo. I had made money – not a great deal, but quite enough for me; and I had been thinking of all kinds of ways of enjoying myself. My father had taken me out to Africa at the age of six, and I had never been home since; so there was something mysterious and attractive about England, and I intended to stay there for the rest of my days.

But from the first I was disappointed with it. In about a week I was tired of seeing sights, and in less than a month I had had enough of restaurants, theatres and race-meetings. I had no real friend to go about with, which probably explains things. Plenty of people invited me to their houses but they didn't seem much interested in me. They would ask me a question or two about South Africa, and then get on to their own affairs. Here was I, thirty-seven years old, strong and healthy, with enough money to have a good time, tired out with nothing to do all day long, so I had just about decided to get back to Africa.

That afternoon I had been in the City on business, and on my way home went into my club to read the evening papers. They were full of the trouble in the Near East, and there was an article about Karolides, the Greek Prime Minister. I rather liked the fellow. From all accounts he seemed the one

1

big man in politics in that part of the world; and he was honest, too, which was more than could be said for most of them. I understood that they hated him in Berlin and Vienna, but that we were going to support him, and one paper said that he was the only barrier between Europe and a World War.

About six o'clock I went home, dressed, dined at the Café Royal, and went to a music hall. It was a stupid show, and I did not stay long. The night was fine and clear as I walked back to the flat I had rented near Portland Place. I envied the crowds of people all round me, talking busily. These shop-girls and clerks, well-dressed young men and policemen, all had some interest in life. I determined to wait for one more day in England; and if nothing happened, I would take the next ship to the Cape.

My flat was on the first floor of a new block. There was a common staircase, with a porter and a liftman at the entrance, but there was no restaurant and each flat was quite shut off from the others. I dislike having servants in the house, so I had a fellow to look after me who came in by the day. He arrived before eight every morning and used to depart at seven in the evening, for I never dined at home.

I was just fitting my key into the door when I noticed a man beside me. I had not seen him coming, and the sudden appearance made me jump. He was a small thin man, with a short brown beard and small, sharp blue eyes. I recognised him as the man from the flat on the top floor, to whom I had said good morning sometimes on the stairs.

'Can I speak to you?' he said. 'May I come in for a minute?' He kept his voice steady with an effort and he kept his hand on my arm.

I got my door open, and with a motion of my hand told him to go in. As soon as he was inside he ran to my back room, where I used to smoke and write my letters. Then he hurried back.

'Is the door locked?' he asked feverishly, and he fastened the chain with his own hand.

'I am very sorry,' he said humbly. 'I know it is rude of

2

me, but you look the kind of man who would understand. I've had you in my mind all this week when things got troublesome. Say, will you do me a favour?'

'I'll listen to you,' I said. 'That's all I'll promise.' I was getting worried by the little fellow's strange behaviour.

'I beg your pardon,' he said. 'I'm a bit confused tonight. You see, I happen at this moment to be dead.'

I sat down in an armchair and lit my pipe.

'What does it feel like?' I asked. I was fairly certain that I had to deal with a madman.

A smile came for a moment to his pale face. 'I'm not mad – yet. Say, sir, I've been watching you, and I believe you are not easily frightened. I think, too, you're an honest man, and ready to face danger if necessary. I am going to take you into my confidence. I need help more than any man ever needed it, and I want to know if I can depend on you.'

'Get on with your story', I said, 'and I'll tell you.'

He seemed to pull himself together with a great effort, and started telling the strangest story. I didn't understand it at first, and had to stop him and ask questions. But here it is, in short:

He was an American, from Kentucky, and after college, being fairly rich, he had started out to see the world. He wrote a bit for the papers, and sent them reports of the Balkan War, and he had spent a year or two in south-eastern Europe. It seemed he spoke foreign languages well, and had got to know many of the important people in those parts. He spoke familiarly of many names that I remembered having seen in the newspapers.

He had played about with politics, at first for the interest of them and then because he couldn't help it. He seemed to me a sharp, restless fellow, who always wanted to get down to the roots of things. He got a little further down than he wanted.

I am giving you what he told me as well as I could understand it. Away behind all the governments and armies there was a big underground movement going on, controlled by very dangerous people. He had discovered it by accident; it

3

attracted him; he went further, and then he got caught. The men in this secret movement were the sort of people who cause revolutions against the government, but there were also rich men who hoped to make money if war broke out. It suited the purposes of both groups to cause a big war in Europe.

The aim of the movement was to cause a quarrel between Russia and Germany. When I asked why, he said the first group thought this would give them their chance to overthrow existing governments, and set up new ones. The second group would make fortunes, for they had no conscience and no fatherland.

I couldn't help saying that there did not seem at present much hope of success in this plan, for Europe was at peace.

'Yes and no,' he said. 'Their plans have been upset to some extent, but they have not been beaten yet. They are keeping back their next and most important action, but if I can keep alive for a month, I shall be able to prevent it.'

'But I thought you were dead,' I put in.

He smiled. 'I'm coming to that, but I must explain a lot of things first. If you read your newspaper, I guess you know the name of Constantine Karolides?'

I sat up at that, for I had been reading about him that very afternoon.

'He is the man who has wrecked all their plans. He is the one big brain in this political business, and he happens also to be an honest man. Therefore he has been on their list for the past twelve months. I found that out, which wasn't difficult, for any fool could guess as much. But I found out the way they were going to kill him, and that knowledge was dangerous. That's why I have had to die.'

I was getting interested in the little fellow, and he went on: 'They can't get him in his own country, for he is well guarded, but on June 15th he is coming to London to an international meeting, and they intend that he shall never return.'

'That's simple enough,' I said. 'You can warn him and keep him at home.'

4

'If he doesn't come,' he replied, 'they will win, for he's the only man who can settle the problems to be discussed at the meeting.'

'What about the British Government?' I asked. 'They are not going to let their guests be murdered. Tell them what you know, and they'll take extra care.'

'No good. If they doubled the police, Constantine would still be killed. My friends are far too clever. But the murder will not happen if there's a certain man who knows all about the matter alive right here in London on June 15th. And that man is I, Franklin P. Scudder.'

Scudder then explained how he had found all this out, and how he himself had been discovered by the secret band, who were now on his track.

'One morning,' he said, 'I saw a man in the street outside this block. I used to stay in my room all day, and only slip out after dark for an hour or two. I watched him for a bit from my window, and I thought I recognised him. The porter says he came in and asked about me. When I came back from my walk last night, I found a card in my letterbox. It had on it the name of the man I want least to meet in the world.'

I think that the look in my companion's eyes, the fear on his face, completed my certainty of his honesty. My own voice was excited as I asked him what he did next.

'I realised I was trapped like a rat, and that there was only one way out. It was no use trying to escape from these men, so I had to die. If they knew I was dead they would pay no more attention to me.'

I asked him how he had managed to make them think he was dead. He smiled. Then he told me how he had got a dead body, dressed it in his own night clothes and put it in his bed. He had first sent away his servant, telling him he was ill. As the dead man's face was not very like his, he had shot it away, and left the gun beside the bed, to make it appear that he had shot himself.

'It wasn't any use,' Scudder continued, 'trying to get into the streets, so I watched from my window till I saw you come

5

home, and then slipped down the stairs to meet you . . . There, sir, I think you know as much as I do of the business.'

By this time I was fairly certain he was speaking the truth, although it was the strangest sort of story. I had made a practice of judging a man rather than his story. If he had only wanted to get into my flat, he would have told a simpler story, more easily believed.

'Hand me your key,' I said, 'and I'll have a look at the dead body. I must be sure that you are speaking the truth.'

He shook his head. 'I guessed you'd ask for that, but I haven't got it. It's on the chain on my dressing table. I had to leave it behind, for fear of suspicion. These men who are after me are clever, you know. You'll have to trust me for tonight, and tomorrow you'll get proof of the death.'

I thought for a moment or two. 'Right. I'll trust you for the night. I'll lock you into this room, and keep the key. Just one word, Mr Scudder. I believe you're honest, but if you are not, I should warn you that I am very quick with a gun.'

I woke next morning to hear my servant, Paddock, making a noise at the smoking room door.

'Stop that noise, Paddock,' I said. 'There's a friend of mine asleep in there. Get breakfast for two and then come and speak to me.'

I told Paddock a story to keep him quiet, and after breakfast, I left Scudder with the newspapers and went down to the City till lunch-time. When I got back, the liftman looked very excited.

'Bad accident here this morning, sir. The gentleman in No 15 has shot himself. The police are up there now.'

I went up to No 15 and found the police making an examination. When I asked questions, they told me to mind my own business, so I spoke to Scudder's servant, and I found he suspected nothing. I went to the inquiry next day, and it was decided that Scudder had shot himself for unknown reasons. I went home and told Scudder about it, and he was very interested. He said he wished he could have been at the inquiry himself.

For two days Scudder stayed quietly in my flat. On the third he seemed to become afraid – not for himself, but for the success of his plan. He said he would tell me more about his story, so that if he were killed, I could take his place.

I did not give him very close attention. The fact is, I was more interested in his own adventures than in his high politics. I considered that Karolides and his affairs were not my business, leaving all that to him. So a lot that he said slipped out of my memory. I remember that he was very clear that the danger to Karolides would not begin till he had got to London, and would come from the highest places where there would be no thought of suspicion. He mentioned the name of a woman, Julia Czechenyi, as having something to do with the danger. He talked, too, of a Black Stone and a man that lisped in his speech, and he described very particularly an old man with a young voice, who could lower his eyelids in the way some birds do.

Next day he was more cheerful and spent the time reading. I went out to dinner in the evening with a mining engineer I had got to see on business and came back about half-past ten. I pushed open the smoking room door, and found the lights were not lit, which struck me as strange. I wondered if Scudder had already gone to bed.

I turned on the light, but there was nobody there. Then I saw something in the far corner of the room that made me go cold with fear.

My guest was lying there on his back, and he was fastened to the floor with a long knife through his heart.

2. The milkman sets out on his travels

I sat down in an armchair and felt very sick. That lasted for maybe five minutes, and was followed by fear and trembling. The poor white face on the floor was more than I could bear, and I managed to get a tablecloth and cover it. I had seen men die violently before; indeed I had killed a few myself in war in South Africa; but murder like this indoors was different. However, I managed to become calm again, and looked at my watch. It was half-past ten.

An idea seized me, and I searched the flat carefully. There was nobody there, nor any sign of anybody, but I shut the windows and locked the door and put the chain on.

By this time my mind was coming back to me, and I could think again. It took me about an hour to go over the whole thing; and I did not hurry, for unless the murderer came back, I had till about six o'clock in the morning for my thoughts.

I was in a terribly difficult position – that much was clear. Any doubt I might have had about the truth of Scudder's story was now gone. The proof of it was lying under the tablecloth. The men who knew that he knew what he knew had found him, and taken the best way to make certain of his silence. Yes; but he had been in my rooms four days, and his enemies must have supposed that he had taken me into his confidence. So I would be the next to go. It might be that very night, or next day, or the day after, but my fate was certain.

Then suddenly I thought of another probability. Supposing I went out now and called in the police, or went to bed and let Paddock find the body and call them in the morning. What kind of a story was I to tell about Scudder? I had lied to Paddock about him, and the whole thing looked very suspicious. If I confessed and told the police everything he had told me, they would simply laugh at me. The chances

8

were a thousand to one that I would be charged with the murder, and it would be easy to prove it. Few people knew me in England; I had no real friend who could come forward and swear to my character. Perhaps that was what those secret enemies were depending on. They were clever enough for anything, and an English prison was as good a way of getting rid of me till after June 15th as a knife in my chest.

Besides, if I told the whole story, and by any chance was believed, I should be doing what they wanted. Karolides would stay at home, and their plans for causing war would succeed. Somehow the sight of Scudder's dead face had made me an even firmer believer in his story. He was gone, but he had taken me into his confidence, and I felt I had to carry on his work.

You may think this foolish for a man in danger of his life, but that was the way I looked at it. I am an ordinary sort of fellow, not braver than other people, but I hate to see a good man overcome, and that long knife would not be the end of Scudder if I could take his place.

It took me an hour or two to think this out, and by that time I had come to a decision. I must disappear somehow, and keep hidden till the end of the second week in June. Then I must somehow find a way to tell the government what Scudder had told me. I wished he had told me more, and that I had listened more carefully to what he had actually said. I knew nothing but a few facts. There was a big risk that, even if I escaped the other dangers, I would not be believed in the end. I must take my chance of that, and hope that something might happen which would prove my story in the eyes of the government.

My first duty was to keep alive for the next three weeks. It was now May 24th, and that meant twenty days of hiding before I dare speak to anyone in authority. I supposed that two sets of people would be looking for me – Scudder's enemies to put me out of existence, and the police, who would want me for Scudder's murder. It was going to be an exciting hunt, and it was strange how the thought of it com-

9

forted me. I had had nothing to do for so long that any chance of activity was welcome. When I had to sit alone with that dead body and merely wait, I was no better than a crushed worm, but if my neck's safety was to depend on my own cleverness I was ready to be cheerful about it.

My next thought was whether Scudder had any papers on him to give me any key to the business. I drew back the tablecloth and searched his pockets, for I had no longer any fear of the body. The face was wonderfully calm for a man who had been struck down in a moment. There was nothing of importance in the pockets and no sign of the little black book in which I had seen him making notes. That no doubt had been taken by the murderer.

But as I looked up from my work I saw that some drawers had been pulled out in the writing table. Scudder would never have left them in that state, for he was the tidiest of men. Someone must have been searching for something – perhaps for the notebook.

I went round the flat again, and found that everything had been upset – the inside of books, drawers, cupboards, boxes, even the pockets of my clothes hanging up in my room. There was no sign of the book. Most likely the enemy had found it, but they had not found it on Scudder's body.

Then I got out a map of the British Isles. My idea was to get off to some wild district, where my experience in Africa would be of some use to me, for I would be like a trapped rat in a city. I considered that Scotland would be best, for my family were Scottish, and I could pass anywhere as an ordinary Scotsman. At first I thought of being a German tourist as I knew the language well, but I decided that to be a Scot would make it easier to pass unnoticed.

The nearest wild part of Scotland was Galloway, and I saw from the time-table that a train left London at 7.10 a.m. which would get me to any Galloway station in the late afternoon. The difficulty was, how was I to reach the London station? I was quite sure that Scudder's friends would be waiting outside, watching for me. Then I had a bright idea, on which I went to bed and slept for two troubled hours.

I got up and dressed at four o'clock, putting on an old suit and some strong walking boots. I had drawn a good amount of gold from the bank two days before, in case Scudder should want money, and I took £50 of it in a belt which I had brought back from South Africa.

Now came the next step. Paddock used to arrive every morning at seven-thirty punctually and let himself in with his own key. But about twenty minutes to seven, as I knew from bitter experience, the milkman came with a great noise of cans, and put my share outside my door. I had seen that milkman sometimes when I had gone out for an early ride on horseback. He was a young man about my own height and he wore a white overall. On him I decided to risk all my chances.

I had a poor breakfast of some dry bread, and then went to get some tobacco to light my pipe. It was kept in a box on the table, and as I put my fingers in, they touched something hard. I drew out Scudder's little black notebook.

That seemed to me a good sign for the future. I lifted the cloth from the body and was astonished at the peace of the dead face.

'Goodbye, old fellow,' I said. 'I am going to do my best for you. Wish me well, wherever you are.'

Then I waited for the milkman. Six-thirty passed, then six-forty, but still he did not come. The fool had chosen this day of all days to be late.

At last at a quarter to seven I heard the noise of cans outside. I opened the door, and then the man jumped a bit at the sight of me.

'Come in here for a moment,' I said. 'I want a word with you.' And I led him into the dining room.

'Will you do me a favour?' I asked. 'Lend me your cap and overall for ten minutes, and here's a pound for you.'

His eyes opened at the sight of the gold, and he smiled broadly. 'What's the idea?' he asked.

'It's a trick on a friend of mine.' I said. 'I haven't time to explain, but I must be a milkman for the next ten minutes. All you've got to do is to stay here till I come back. You'll

11

be a bit late, but nobody will complain, and you'll have that pound for yourself.'

'All right,' he said cheerfully. 'I'm not a man to spoil a joke. Here are the things, sir.'

I put on his flat blue hat and his white overall, picked up the cans, shut my door loudly and went whistling downstairs. The porter told me to stop that noise, which sounded as if my appearance was satisfactory.

At first I thought there was nobody in the street, but then I caught sight of a man walking slowly along on the other side. I happened to notice the window of the house opposite, and saw a face. The two men seemed to exchange a signal.

I crossed the street, whistling gaily and imitating the walk of the milkman. Then I turned a corner and found myself in an empty street. I at once dropped the cans on a piece of waste ground and threw the hat and overall after them. I had only just put on my cloth cap when a postman came round the corner. I gave him good morning and he answered unsuspiciously. At that moment a neighbouring church clock struck the hour of seven.

There was not a second to lose. As soon as I got into the busy station road, I began to run. It was ten past by the station clock as I got there, and I had no time to get a ticket. Besides, I had not even decided on a place to go to. A porter showed me where the train for Scotland was leaving. It was already moving. Two station officials tried to stop me, but I was able to get past them and climb into the last carriage. Three minutes later, an angry guard was writing me out a ticket.

So I entered on my new life. I could hardly believe that a week ago I had been finding the world dull.

3. The adventure of the literary innkeeper

I had a dull time travelling north that day. It was fine May weather, and I asked myself why, when I was still a free man, I had stayed on in London instead of coming out into the country. I didn't dare go into the dining car, but I got a lunch-basket at Leeds. I also got the morning papers which said that affairs in the Balkans were very peaceful.

When I had done with them, I got out Scudder's little black notebook and studied it. It was filled with notes mostly figures, though now and then a name was printed in, Now I was certain that Scudder never did anything without a reason, and I was sure that there was a cipher in all this.

That is a subject that has always interested me, and I did some work at it during the war in South Africa. I have a good mind for puzzles and things of that sort, and I used to consider myself rather clever at finding out ciphers. This one appeared to have figures instead of letters, but usually anyone with common sense can find the key to a cipher of this kind after an hour or two's work. I didn't think Scudder would have been satisfied with anything so easy, so I set to work on the printed words, for you can make a good cipher with figures if you have a key word to tell you in what order the letters come.

I worked for hours, but none of the words gave me the key. Then I fell asleep, and woke at Dumfries just in time to get out of the train and catch the slow one going to Galloway. About five o'clock the carriage was empty, the farmers having all got out, so I left the train myself at a small station in the heart of the moor. No one except the old station master and his child, who took my ticket, was there as I left the station and set forth along a white road across the brown moor.

It was a beautiful spring evening, with every hill showing

13

clearly, and the fresh air full of the smell of the moor. It had the strangest effect on my spirits. I actually felt happy, as if I was a boy on holiday, instead of a man of thirty-seven wanted by the police. I felt as I used to feel when starting a long journey on a cold morning in Africa. I walked along the road whistling, without any plan, but just wanting to go on and on.

It was some hours since I tasted food, and I was feeling very hungry when I came to a shepherd's cottage up a path near a stream. The man and his wife welcomed me with the true kindness of country people. They gave me a good meal and offered me a bed, which I was glad to accept after such a tiring day. I never opened my eyes till five the next morning, when their work started again.

They refused any payment, and by six I was on the road going south again. My idea was to return to the railway line a station or two farther on than the place where I had got out the day before, and then go back the way I had come for some distance. This would make it difficult for the police to keep on my track, for they would naturally suppose that I was going farther away from London, perhaps in the direction of a seaport.

I walked up over the moor until from a high place I could see the valley, and there, a mile away, I saw the smoke of a train. I went down to the station, which fortunately was a very small one, and bought a ticket for Dumfries. The train came and I got into a carriage where the only passenger was a shepherd, fast asleep. He had his dog with him, an ugly animal with one eye that I mistrusted. On the seat was a morning paper, and I read all about the Portland Place murder, as it was called.

My man, Paddock, had called the police, and they arrested the milkman. Poor fellow, he was having a bad time for the pound I had given him; but, for me, he had been cheap at the price, for he had taken up the time and attention of the police most of the day. They had set him free at last, as they believed the real criminal had escaped by train to the north. It was not said that they suspected me, but I felt sure they did.

There was nothing else in the paper, nothing about foreign politics or Karolides, or the things that interested Scudder. I laid it down, and found that we were arriving at the station where I had got out the day before. The train going west was waiting to let us pass, and I saw three men get down from it and ask the station master questions. I supposed they were local police, ordered by Scotland Yard in London to make inquiries, and they had tracked me as far as this station. The child pointed up the road that I had gone, and one of the men wrote something in a notebook. They all looked up the road, but I did not see if they set out to follow me that way, for our train left the station, going east.

Soon afterwards, the train stopped by a small bridge. I looked out. Every window was closed and there was no one anywhere in sight, so I quickly opened the door and jumped down into some bushes which grew along the line. It would have been all right but for that dog. Thinking that I was trying to get away with its master's belongings, it started to make such a noise that it woke up the shepherd, who stood at the carriage door shouting. He seemed to think I was trying to kill myself. I crept through the bushes for a hundred yards or so, and then looked back. The guard and several passengers were standing by the open door and looking in my direction. Instead of leaving secretly, I had thus drawn the attention of the whole train, and it would not be long before the police heard about it. Soon afterwards the train started off, and I was alone.

All round me was empty moorland, with some hills to the north. Although there was not a human being in sight, strangely enough I felt for the first time the fear of the hunted. It was not the police I thought of, but the other people, who knew that I knew Scudder's secret and dared not let me live. I was certain they would come after me with a greater determination that the British law, and once they caught me I should find no mercy.

I went along as quickly as I could over the moor towards the northern hills, and did not rest till I was high up and could see all round me. There was nothing moving anywhere, but suddenly in the sky I caught sight of something that made my heart beat rapidly.

Low down in the south an aeroplane was rising into the sky. I was as certain as if I had been told that that aeroplane was looking for me, and that it did not belong to the police. I watched it from the shelter of a bush as it flew low over the hilltops, and then in circles over the valley up which I had come. After a time it rose to a great height and flew away back to the south. I did not like this searching from the air, and began to think less well of the place I had chosen to hide in. There were no trees or houses where I could hide if my enemies were in the air. I decided to find a better place.

About six in the evening I came out of the moorland, and reached a bridge near a lonely house. A young man was leaning on the wall of the bridge smoking a pipe and looking at the water below.

'Good evening to you,' he said. 'It's a fine night for the road.'

The smell of roast meat came from the house, and I was hungry.

'Is that an inn?' I asked.

'At your service,' he said politely. 'I am the landlord, sir, and I hope you will stay the night, for to tell you the truth I have had no company for a week. It's a dull life here. What I need is excitement and adventure, so that I can write books.'

I told him that adventure had come to me already, and I then invented a story about a band of criminals who had followed me from South Africa and were now on my tracks. I said that they had killed my best friend and were now trying to kill me, but that the police were after them.

'You believe me?' I asked.

'Of course I do,' he replied, and held out his hand. 'I believe everything out of the common. The only thing to distrust is the usual.'

He was very young, but he was the man to help me.

'I think,' I went on, 'that they are off my track for a moment, but I must lie hidden for a day or two. Can you take me in?'

16

He took my arm in his eagerness and drew me towards the house.

'You can hide here as safely as anywhere,' he said, 'and I'll see that nobody talks. You'll tell me some more of your adventures, won't you?'

As I entered the inn I heard from far off the noise of an engine. There in the western sky was my friend, the aeroplane.

Next day I stayed in my room on the first floor, and spent the time studying Scudder's cipher. I could not solve it, but about three o'clock I had a sudden idea. The name Julia Czechenyi flashed into my mind. Scudder had said it was the key to the Karolides business; perhaps it was the keyword to the cipher. I soon saw that it was, and in half an hour I was reading with a white face and fingers tapping on the table.

As I looked out of the window, I saw a big open motor car coming up the road to the inn. It drew up at the door, and two men got out. Ten minutes later the innkeeper slipped into my room, his eyes bright with excitement.

'There are two fellows below looking for you,' he whispered. 'They are having a drink in the dining room. They asked about you and said they hoped to meet you here. Oh! they described you well, down to your boots and shirt. I told them you had been here last night and had gone off on a motor bicycle this morning. One of them swore at that.'

I made him tell me what they looked like. One was a dark-eyed thin fellow, the other was always smiling and lisped in his talk. He did not think they were foreigners. I took a bit of paper and wrote these words in German, as if they were part of a letter:

'. . . Black Stone. Scudder knew this, but could not act for a week or two. I don't think I can do any good now, especially as Karolides is uncertain about his plans. But if Mr T advises, I will do the best I . . .'

I made it look like a loose page of a private letter. 'Take this down and say it was found in my bedroom, and ask

17

them to return it to me if they pass me on the road.'

Three minutes later I heard the car start, and looking from behind the curtain caught sight of two figures, one thin, the other fat and well dressed. The car drove off rapidly, and the innkeeper appeared in great excitement.

'Your paper woke them up,' he said, laughing. 'The dark fellow went as white as death, and the fat one whistled and looked terribly angry.'

I laughed too. Then I asked him to call the police, for I knew the two men would return when they didn't find me anywhere on the road.

About eight next morning three police officers arrived, and twenty minutes later I saw from my window a second car coming in the opposite direction. It did not come up to the inn, but stopped two hundred yards away in the shelter of some trees. The driver carefully turned it round before he and the other man left it. A moment or two later I heard their steps at the inn door.

My plan had been to lie hidden in my room and see what happened. I had an idea that if I could bring the police and my other more dangerous enemies together, something might happen to my advantage. But now I saw something better to do. I wrote a line of thanks to my host, opened the window and dropped quietly into a bush. Unseen, I crossed the road, went round the trees and came to the car. I started the engine, jumped in and drove away. I thought I heard behind me the sound of angry voices.

4. The adventure of the young politician

You may picture me driving that powerful car as quickly as it would go over the moor roads on that shining May morning; looking back at first over my shoulder and then forward to the next turn in the road; then driving with a
18

wandering eye, just awake enough to keep straight. For I was thinking with despair of what I had found in Scudder's notebook.

The little man had told me a lot of lies. All his stories about the Balkans and revolutions and so on were nonsense, and so was Karolides. And yet not quite, as you shall hear. I had got myself into my present position through believing him, and had been deceived. Here was his book telling me a different story, and instead of being distrustful, I believed it absolutely.

June 15th was going to be an important day – far more important than Scudder had told me. It was so big that I didn't blame him for keeping the truth secret. He wanted to manage everything by himself, that was clear, for he had found it all out by himself. It was risks after all that he was chiefly greedy about.

The whole story was in notes, but only the outline, and a strange expression that came half a dozen times: 'Thirty-nine steps'. The last time it was used, it was, 'Thirty-nine steps, I counted them. High tide 10.17 p.m.' I could not understand this at all.

I learnt that there was no question of preventing a European war. That was coming, as sure as Fate. It had been arranged ever since 1912. Karolides was going to be the occasion. He was to be killed on June 14th, two weeks and four days from that May morning, and nothing could prevent that.

The second thing was that this war was going to be a great surprise to Britain. Karolides's death would make the Balkan countries quarrel, Austria would interfere and Russia would be annoyed with Austria. There would be angry words, but Germany would pretend to act as peacemaker, then, finding some cause for a quarrel, would suddenly attack us. That was the idea, and a good one. Fair words and then a stroke in the dark. While we were talking about Germany's good intentions, they would secretly surround our coast with mines and submarines so that none of our warships could come safely out of harbour.

But all this depended on a third thing which was to happen on June 15th. On that day a very important man was coming over from Paris to discuss the secret war plans of the British and French Governments, and he was to be given nothing less than a statement of the positions of the British Navy in time of war.

But on June 15th there were to be others in London – others, at whom I could only guess. Scudder called them 'The Black Stone'. They were our deadly enemies, and the information intended for France was to go into their pockets. And it was to be used, remember – used a week later suddenly in the dark of the summer night.

My first thought was to write to the government, but who would believe me? I must show some sign as a proof, and God alone knew what sign I could show. Above all, I must keep alive, and that was not going to be so easy with all the police of Britain as well as the Black Stone close on my track.

I drove east for a long way, and about midday entered a village, where I thought I would stop and eat. As I went slowly down the street I saw the post office, and a policeman at the door reading a telegram. When he saw me, he raised his hand and told me to stop. I was nearly stupid enough to obey, till it flashed on me that the telegram had to do with me. I set off as quickly as I could. The policeman tried to jump on the car, but got a blow in the eye from me and fell back.

It was clear the main roads were no place for me, for it was easy for the police to telegraph to all the villages through which I was likely to pass. So I turned off into by-roads, but it was difficult without a map, and I began to see what a fool I had been to steal the car, for the big green machine would be recognised anywhere. If I left it to go on foot, it would be discovered in an hour or two, and I should get no start in the race.

After a time, I heard a noise in the sky, and there was that devil of an aeroplane a dozen miles away and coming rapidly towards me! In this moorland I was at its mercy; my only chance to escape was to get into a leafy valley where I might shelter. Down the hill I went as fast as I dared till I came to a small wood.

Suddenly on my left I heard the sound of another car, and realised with a shock that I was just up to a gate, where a private road came out on to mine. I tried to stop but it was too late. Another car was already across my path. In another second there would have been a terrible accident. I did the only thing possible, and ran straight through the bushes on my right, trusting that there would be something soft on the other side.

But there I was mistaken. My car went through the bushes like butter, then fell forwards. There was a deep stream bed fifty feet below. I tried to jump out, and by good luck a branch of a tree caught me by the chest, lifted me up and held me while the car fell with a loud crash down into the stream.

The driver of the other car came to my rescue and was very kind. When I told him that my name was Twisdon and I was on holiday, he took me to his house and invited me to stay for the night.

'You'll need time to make arrangements about your car,' he said. 'And while you're here, perhaps you can help me, Mr Twisdon. I'm hoping to get elected to parliament, and I'm holding a meeting tonight at Brattleburn. An important man who was coming to make a speech has telegraphed that he's ill and can't come. I can't speak for more than ten minutes myself. I wonder if you can help me? They're expecting a stranger, and nobody will know you.'

'All right,' I said, 'I'm not much good as a speaker, but I'll tell them a bit about places I've been to, if you like.'

At my words his troubles all disappeared, and he was full of gratitude. He lent me a coat, and never thought of asking why I had been out driving a car without one. As we drove to Brattleburn he told me about his life. I was glad to learn one fact – that he had an uncle who was a minister in the government. As we passed through a little town two police-men signalled us to stop, and flashed their lamps on us.

'I beg your pardon, Sir Harry,' said one. 'We've orders to look for a car.'

'All right,' said my host, and I silently thanked God for the strange way I had been brought to safety.

At the meeting Sir Harry made a poor speech, telling the five hundred people there that the talk of Germany being our enemy was nonsense, and if he were in parliament he would try to spend less on the navy and spend more on social work instead. I made a speech about life in Australia. It had nothing to do with politics but the audience liked it.

When we were in the car again my host was in great spirits at the success of the meeting.

'Now, Twisdon,' he said, 'you're coming home with me. I'm all alone, and if you'll stop a day or two I'll show you some good fishing.'

After a pleasant supper I thought the time had come for me to speak openly. I saw by this man's eye that he was the kind you can trust.

'Listen, Sir Harry,' I said. 'I've something important to say to you. You're a good fellow, and I'm going to say what I think. Where did you get that nonsense you talked tonight?'

'Was it as bad as that?' he asked sorrowfully. 'I thought it was rather weak myself. I got it from various papers and books. But you surely don't think Germany would ever go to war with us?'

'Ask that question in six weeks and it won't need an answer,' I said. 'If you'll give me your attention for half an hour I am going to tell you a story.'

I can still see that bright room and Sir Harry standing restlessly by the fireplace while I lay back in an armchair, speaking. It was the first time I had ever told anyone the exact truth, so far as I understood it, and it did me good, for it straightened out the thing in my own mind. I missed no detail. He heard all about Scudder, the milkman, the note-book and my doings in Galloway. He got very excited and walked up and down.

'So you see,' I ended, 'you have got here in your house the man that is wanted for the Portland Place murder. Your duty is to send your car for the police and give me up. I don't think I'll get very far. The Black Stone will manage an accident, and I'll have a knife in my chest at once. But that's your duty. Perhaps in a month's time you'll be sorry, but you have no cause to think of that.'

He was looking at me with bright, steady eyes. 'What was your work in South Africa, Mr Hannay?' he asked.

'Mining engineer,' I said.

'Not the sort of profession that weakens a man's courage, is it?'

I laughed. 'I'm not easily frightened, if that's what you mean.' I took down a hunting knife I saw on the wall, threw it up and caught it in my lips. That needs a steady heart.

He watched me with a smile. 'I don't want proofs. I may be a poor politician, but I can judge a man's character all right. You're no murderer and no fool, and I believe you are speaking the truth. I'm going to help you. Now, what can I do?'

'First, I want you to write to your uncle in the government. I must find a way to get in touch with the government before June 15th.'

'That won't help you. This is Foreign Office business, and my uncle would have nothing to do with it. Besides, he would never believe it. No, I'll do better. I'll write to the Permanent Secretary at the Foreign Office. He's a sort of relation, and a very good fellow. What do you want me to say?'

He sat down at a table and wrote what I told him. If a man called Twisdon came to see the Permanent Secretary, would the latter listen to what he had to say? Twisdon would prove who he was by using the words 'Black Stone' and whistling the tune 'Annie Laurie'.

'You'll find my relation – his name is Sir Walter Bullivant – at his country cottage at Artinswell. Good, that's done. What's the next thing?'

'You're about my height. Lend me an old suit. Then show me a map of the district and explain what the land is like round here. Lastly, if the police come looking for me, just show them the car in the stream. If the Black Stone appear, tell them I went south by train after your meeting.'

He promised to do all these things, and I went off to sleep for a few hours in the armchair. At two o'clock in the morning he wakened me and led me out into the starry night. He gave me an old bicycle and told me which way to go so as to reach the hills by daylight. Then I said goodbye, and rode off.

When the pale morning light showed, I found myself in a wide green world high in the hills, with valleys on every side. Here at any rate I should be able to have early news of my enemies.

5. The adventure of the sick roadman

I sat down where the road passed over the hilltop to examine my position. I could see all round me for miles, but except for the smoke from a cottage half a mile away down the road there was no sign of human life. In the sky the birds sang – and then I heard that hated noise again.

I realised that my position that I had thought so good might in truth be a trap, for there was no shelter anywhere in these bare green places. I sat quite still and hopeless while the aeroplane came, flying high. It dropped several hundred feet and began to circle round the hill. Now it was flying very low, and now the observer caught sight of me. I could see one of the two men looking at me through glasses.

Suddenly it began to rise, and then flew rapidly away till it was a mere dot in the distance.

That made me do some hard thinking. My enemies had found me, and the next thing would be a circle of men surrounding me. The aeroplane had seen my bicycle and would naturally think that I would try to escape by road. In that case there might be a chance on the moors to the right or left.

I walked with the machine a hundred yards from the road and threw it into a deep pool, where it sank out of sight. Then I climbed up to where I could see the road on both sides of the hill. Nothing was moving on it.

As I have said, there was nowhere to hide, and now these free moorlands seemed like prison walls. The sharp hill air was like the breath of the prison itself. I went on and after a time came to another high piece of ground, from which I could see – for my life in Africa had given me extraordinarily sharp eyes – some men two miles away. They were advancing in a line up the hill.

I dropped out of sight behind the sky-line. If that way was shut to me, I must try the other one. I ran hard, keeping as low as possible, but watching the hill before me. I thought I saw some men moving there in front of me. If you are surrounded like this, there is only one means of escape. You must stay where you are, and let your enemies search the place and not find you. That was good sense, but how could I possibly avoid notice in that bare land? I would have buried myself to the neck in mud, or lain below water, or climbed the tallest tree. But there was not the smallest stick, nor any plant big enough to hide me.

Then in a bend of the road, beside a heap of stones, I found the roadman.

He had just arrived – it was soon after seven – and he threw down his hammer as if he was too tired to begin work. He looked at me dully.

'I'm sorry I ever gave up being a shepherd,' he said. 'Then I was my own master. Now I'm a slave to the government, tied to the roadside, with sore eyes and a bent back.'

He picked up his hammer, struck a stone, then dropped the instrument with some bad words, and put his hands to his head.

'What a terrible headache I've got,' he cried. 'I can't work. I'm going back home to bed. The surveyor can do what he likes about it.'

I asked him what the trouble was, though indeed it was clear enough.

25

He explained that his youngest daughter had been married the day before, and he had drunk too much. The surveyor was coming round that morning to see the work done. When he added that the surveyor was a new one and did not know him, I offered to take his place and do his work. And he gladly accepted my offer.

I borrowed his eye-glasses and dirty old hat; took off my coat and collar for him to carry home; borrowed, too, his dirty old pipe. He showed me what work to do, and then went off happily to his cottage to sleep. That may have been his chief purpose, but I think there was also something left in a bottle. I prayed that he might be safe out of sight before my friends arrived on the scene.

Then I set to work to dress for the part. I opened the collar of my shirt and showed my neck, burnt brown by the sun. I got my boots and clothes all white from the dust of the road. I rubbed dirt into my face, and even made my eyes sore with dust. I was not satisfied with my boots, so I kicked them against the stones until they looked rough enough for any roadman. The men after me would miss no detail. Then I had some breakfast off the bread and cheese the roadman had left for me.

There was still no sign of anything on the road as I started working at the stones, carrying them from a big heap a hundred yards away.

I remember a fellow in South Africa once telling me that the secret of playing a part was to think yourself into it. You could never succeed for long, he said, unless you could persuade yourself that you were it. So I shut off all other thoughts, and kept my mind on the road making. I thought of the little cottage as my home. I remembered the years I had been a shepherd . . .

Suddenly a little car came along, and stopped. A round-faced young man looked out and spoke to me.

'Are you Alexander Turnbull, in charge of this part of the road?' he asked.

I said I was.

'I am the new surveyor,' he went on. 'A fair bit of road,

Turnbull, but rather soft a mile further back, and the edges want cleaning. See you look after that. Good day.'

Clearly my appearance was good enough for the surveyor. I went on steadily with my work for some hours. Just about midday a big car came down the hill slowly. It passed me, then stopped. Two men got out as if to stretch their legs, and walked towards me.

They were the men I had seen from the window of the inn – one thin and dark, the other rather fat and smiling. When he spoke, he lisped, and the eyes in his head were as bright and sharp as a bird's.

'Good morning,' said the first. 'Easy work you've got there.'

I had not looked up as they came near, and now when he spoke, I straightened my back painfully in the manner of roadmen, and looked at them steadily before replying. I saw two pairs of eyes that missed nothing.

'There are worse kinds of work, and better,' I said, speaking like an uneducated Scot. 'I would rather have yours, sitting all day on cushions in a car. It's you and your cars that spoil my roads. If we all had our rights you ought to mend what you break.'

The fat one noticed my boots, and with a word in German drew the attention of the dark-eyed man.

'You've a good taste in boots,' he said. 'These were never made by a country shoemaker.'

'They were not,' I agreed. 'They were made in London. I was given them last year by a gentleman up here for the shooting.'

Again the fat one spoke in German. 'Let us get on. This fellow is all right.'

They asked one last question.

'Did you see anyone pass early this morning? He might be on a bicycle or he might be on foot.'

I very nearly fell into the trap and told a story of a bicyclist hurrying past in the grey light before sunrise. But I had the sense to see my danger. I pretended to think deeply.

'I wasn't up very early,' I said. 'You see my daughter was

married last night, and I stayed up late drinking with my friends. I opened the house door about seven this morning, and there was nobody on the road then. Since I began work, there have been only the surveyor, the baker and a shepherd from the village, besides you gentlemen.'

They got into their car and were out of sight in three minutes. My heart became greatly lightened, but I went on just the same with my work. It was lucky I did so, for about ten minutes later the car returned, one of the men waving his hand to me. Those people left nothing to chance.

I finished Turnbull's bread and cheese, and soon I had finished the stones. The next step was what puzzled me. I could not continue this road-making business for long. By the greatest good fortune, Turnbull had stayed indoors so far, but if he appeared on the scene, there would be trouble. I felt sure that my followers were all round, and that if I walked in any direction I should meet with questioners.

I stayed at my post till five o'clock. By that time I had decided to go to Turnbull's cottage when dark came, and take my chance of getting over the hills during the night. But suddenly a new car came up the road, and stopped a yard or two from me. A fresh wind had risen, and the driver wanted to light his pipe.

It was an open touring car with a lot of bags in the back. One man sat in it, and by an astonishing chance I knew him. His name was Marmaduke Jopley, a hateful creature. He made money by persuading rich young lords and foolish old ladies to put money into certain companies. He was well known at big dances and among society of a certain rank. He would almost creep on his stomach to anyone with a nobleman's title. I had met him in London and his boastful talk had made me sick.

Well, there he was now, neatly dressed, in a fine new car. A sudden mad feeling took possession of me, and in a second I had jumped into the car and had him by the shoulder.

'Hello, Jopley,' I cried. 'Well met, my friend!'

He got a fright, and looked at me open-mouthed. 'Who are you?'

28

'My name's Hannay,' I said. 'From South Africa, you remember.'

'Good God, the murderer!' he cried.

'Just so. And there'll be a second murder, my friend, if you don't do as I tell you. Give me that coat of yours. That cap, too.'

He did as I said, for he was trembling with fear. I put his fine driving coat over my dirty shirt, and his cap on my head. The dusty roadman was in a minute changed into one of the neatest motorists in Scotland. On Mr Jopley's head I pushed Turnbull's shapeless old hat and told him to keep it there.

Then I turned the car, for my plan was to go back the way he had come. The watchers having seen it before, would probably let it pass unquestioned.

'Now, my child,' I said, 'sit quite still and be a good boy. I mean you no harm. I'm only borrowing your car for an hour or two. But if you play me any tricks, I'll twist your head off your body.'

I enjoyed that evening ride. We went eight miles down the valley, through a village or two, and I saw several strange-looking men standing about here and there. These were the watchers who would have had much to say to me if I had come in any other dress. As it was, they paid me no attention.

As it became dark, I turned up a by-road towards the moorland hills. When all the houses were left far behind, I stopped in a lonely place, and I turned the car round and gave Jopley his clothes back.

'A thousand thanks,' I said. 'There's more use in you than I thought. Now be off, and find the police if you want to do so.'

6. The strange house on the moor

I spent the night on the hillside in the shelter of a large rock. It was very cold, for I had no coat. This was in Mr Turnbull's keeping, as was Scudder's little book, my watch and – worst of all – my pipe and tobacco. Only my money was with me in my belt.

I got some kind of warmth from the soft plants by the rock. My spirits had risen and I was beginning to enjoy this mad game of being hunted. So far I had been very lucky. The milkman, the literary innkeeper, Sir Harry, the roadman, and that fool Jopley, were all pieces of undeserved good fortune. Somehow the first success gave me a feeling that I was going to win in the end.

My chief trouble was that I was so hungry. I lay and thought of the good food that I had scorned in London, and Paddock's excellent cooking. In wishing hopelessly for these things I fell asleep.

I woke very stiff and cold about an hour after daylight. It took me a little time to remember where I was, for I had been very tired and had slept heavily. I raised myself on my arms and looked down into the valley, and that one look set me putting on my boots in mad haste. For there were men below, not more than a quarter of a mile off, spread out on the hillside like a fan. Jopley had not been slow in looking for his revenge.

I set off up the hill keeping out of sight behind rocks and low bushes, and reached the top undiscovered. Here I showed myself, and was at once seen. I heard cries coming up from below, and saw the direction of the searchers had changed. They were all coming towards me. I went over the top, pretending to go straight on, but when out of sight, I ran hard the other way, and after a time I looked from behind a rock and saw the men all going past me the wrong way.

I went along the edge of a hill so that a deep valley would

be between me and my followers. The exercise had warmed me up and I was beginning to enjoy myself, but I knew very little about the country, and I had no idea of what I was going to do. I trusted to the strength of my legs, but I knew quite well that those behind me would be familiar with the land, and that my lack of knowledge would be a serious difficulty. All round me were hills and moors, and one direction seemed as good as another.

My trick had given me a good start – call it twenty minutes – and I had the width of the valley behind me before I saw again the first heads of the searchers. The police had clearly called in local men to help them, for the men I saw appeared to be shepherds and farmers. They shouted at sight of me, and I waved my hand. Some of them began going down their side of the valley. I felt as if I was taking part in some schoolboy game.

But very soon it began to seem less of a game. Those men were strong fellows and they knew the ground. Looking back, I saw that only three were following me directly, and I guessed that the others were going a shorter way to get in front of me. I began to run faster in an attempt to escape before they reached me, and after a time saw a house in a hollow of the moor in front. It had some trees round it, which seemed to offer some shelter.

As I reached the rough garden of the house, my followers were out of sight for a moment. I went towards it, and saw through an open window an oldish gentleman quietly watching me. There was nothing to be done but to go in. I did so, and walked into a pleasant room, full of books and glass cases with strange coins and ancient tools inside. At a desk with some papers and books open before him, sat the kind-looking old gentleman. His face was round and shining, some big glasses were stuck on his nose, and as for his head, it had as much hair on it as an egg. He never moved as I entered, but looked a bit surprised and waited for me to speak.

It was not easy, with about five minutes to spare, to tell a stranger who I was and what I wanted, and to win his help. I did not attempt it. There was something about the eye of the man before me, something so sharp and full of know-ledge, that I could not find a word. I merely looked at him and hesitated.

'You seem in a hurry, my friend,' he said slowly.

I looked through the window. There was a view across the moor and some men could be seen half a mile away. He took up a pair of big glasses and examined the figures patiently.

'Escaping from justice, eh?'

I made a motion with my head.

'We'll go into the matter later,' he said. 'I don't like my private affairs being interrupted by stupid country policemen. Go into the next room, and close the door. You will be perfectly safe.'

And this extraordinary man took up his pen again.

I found myself in a small dark room. The door shut behind me with a noise like the door of a safe. Once again I was unexpectedly saved. All the same, I was not comfortable in mind. There was something puzzling, even frightening, about the old gentleman. He had been too easy and ready, almost as if he expected me. And his eyes had been terribly clever.

No sound came to me in that dark place. Perhaps the police were searching the house. I tried to forget how hungry I was. Then the door opened, and I came into the sunlight of the room again.

'Have they gone?' I asked.

'They have gone,' said the master of the house. 'I persuaded them that you had crossed the hill. I do not choose that the police should come between me and one to whom I am delighted to show honour. This is a lucky morning for you, Mr Hannay.'

As he spoke his eyelids seemed to tremble and fall a little over his sharp grey eyes. In a flash the words of Scudder came back to me. He said, 'He could lower his eyelids in the way some birds do.' Then I saw that I had walked into the enemies' camp.

My first thought was to kill the old fellow with my hands,

and escape. He seemed to understand my intention, for he smiled gently, and pointed behind me. I turned, and saw two men-servants aiming guns at me.

He knew my name, but he had never seen me before. As the thought passed my mind, I saw a faint chance.

'I don't know what you mean,' I said roughly. 'And who are you calling Hannay? My name's Ainslie.'

'So?' he said, still smiling. 'But of course you have others. We won't quarrel about a name.'

I was beginning to get my senses back now, and I thought that my dress, and having no coat or collar, would at least not show who I really was. I put on an angry expression.

'I suppose you're going to give me up after all. A nice trick to play, isn't it? I wish I had never seen that motor car! Here's the money, if that's what you want,' and I threw four pounds on the table.

He opened his eyes a little. 'Oh, no, I shall not give you up. My friends and I have a little private matter to settle with you, that is all. You know a little too much, Mr Hannay. You are a clever actor, but not quite clever enough.'

He spoke as if he was sure of himself, but I could see the beginning of doubt in his mind.

'Oh, stop talking nonsense,' I cried. 'Everything's against me. I haven't had a bit of luck since I came on shore from my ship at Leith. What's the harm in a poor fellow with an empty stomach picking up some money he finds in a broken motor car? That's all I've done, and for that I've been hunted for two days by those devils of policemen over these hills. You can do what you like, sir. Ned Ainslie's finished; he can't fight any more.'

I could see that the doubt was increasing.

'Will you please tell me the story of your recent doings?' he asked.

'I can't, sir,' I said with the voice of a beggar. 'I've not had a bite to eat for two days. Give me a mouthful of food, and then I'll tell you the truth.'

I must have shown my hunger in my face, for he signalled to one of his men. He brought me some cold meat, and I swallowed it like an animal. In the middle of the meal he spoke suddenly to me in German, but I looked up surprised as if I didn't understand it.

Then I told him my story – how I had come on shore at Leith a week ago, and was going overland to my brother at Wigtown. I had no money, and when I saw a big motor car lying in a stream, I climbed down to see what had happened, and had found four pounds lying on the floor. I took the money, but somehow the law had got after me, and I had been hunted ever since.

'You're a good liar, Hannay,' he said, when I'd finished.

I got very angry. 'Stop fooling! I tell you my name's Ned Ainslie, and I never heard of anyone called Hannay in my life. I'd rather have the police than you playing these tricks. No, sir, I beg your pardon, I don't mean that. I'm thankful to you for the meal, and I'd like to go now the police are out of the way.'

It was clear he was very puzzled. You see he had never seen me, and my appearance must have changed a lot from my photographs, if he had got one.

'I don't propose to let you go. If you are what you say you are, you will soon have a chance to prove it. If you are what I believe you are, I do not think you will see the light much longer.'

He rang a bell, and a third servant appeared.

'I want the car in five minutes,' he said. 'There will be three to lunch.'

Then he looked steadily at me, and that was the hardest thing of all to bear. There was something of the devil in those eyes, cold and terribly clever. But I managed to look back at him, and even smiled.

'You'll know me next time, sir,' I said.

'Karl,' he spoke in German to one of the men, 'you will put this fellow in the store room till I return. You will be responsible to me for his safe keeping.'

I was marched out of the room with a gun on each side of me.

*

34

The store room was a damp dark room with no carpet on the floor, and nothing to sit on. By feeling about with my hands, I found that boxes, bags and barrels surrounded the walls. There was nothing to do but wait in the dark. The old fellow had gone off to get the men who had spoken to me yesterday, and they would at once remember me, for I was in the same dress. What was a roadman doing twenty miles from his place of work, and hunted by the police? Probably they had seen Turnbull. Jopley, too. It would not be difficult for them to put the true story together. What chance had I in this moorland house against these three and their armed servants?

The two and the old man would be back for lunch, so I hadn't more than two hours to wait. I was afraid, too, and angry that I had been caught like this. I only hoped that I could kill one of them before they killed me. The more I thought, the angrier I grew, and I got up and moved about the room to relieve my feelings. I tried the window, but the covers were too tight to move. I found the boxes impossible to open, and there was nothing of interest in the sacks. Then I found by feeling round the wall the handle of a cupboard. It was locked but I managed to get it open.

There were some strange things inside. The first thing I found was a small electric lamp, which was in good order. This gave me light to see what else there was. There were bottles and packing cases, inside one of which were some little grey bricks. I took up one in my hand and it turned to powder as I crushed it. I smelt it, then tasted it. After that I sat down to think. I hadn't been a mining engineer for nothing, and I knew explosive when I saw it.

With one of these bricks I could blow up the whole house. I had used it in South Africa and knew its power. The trouble was that my knowledge wasn't exact. I had forgotten the proper way of preparing it, and did not know how much to use. Although I had worked with it, I had never handled it with my own fingers.

But it was a chance, the only possible chance. It was a terrible risk, but against it was an absolute black certainty.

If I used it, I should probably blow myself into the tree tops; but if I didn't, I should certainly be lying in a six-foot hole in the garden by the evening. There did not seem much hope either way, but anyhow there was a chance, both for myself and my country.

I was trembling with fear, but I managed to collect enough courage to take a quarter of one of the bricks, and bury it beneath one of the sacks near the door. Then I prepared to light it with some matches I found in my pocket. I made a line of powder across to the window, where I hid behind some of the barrels. What if they contained more explosive? But I couldn't bear to think another moment. The memory of Scudder's dead face decided me, and I struck a match, and said a prayer.

A great wave of heat seemed to rise from the floor. The wall opposite to me flashed into a golden yellow and flew to pieces with a terrible thundering crash. Something dropped on me, hurting my left shoulder. And then I think I became unconscious.

But this lasted only for a few seconds. I could hardly breathe for the thick yellow smoke, and I struggled to my feet through the stones, wood and fallen rubbish. I felt the fresh air coming in where the window frame had been blown out, and I stepped out into the garden, surrounded by clouds of smoke. I felt very sick, but I could move my limbs, and I ran unsteadily away from the house.

There was an old stone dovecot not far off, and I thought if I could get there without leaving tracks I might find a hiding place, for my enemies would naturally think, when they did not find my body in the store room, that I had escaped on to the moor, and would go there to look for me.

Climbing up this dovecot was one of the hardest things I have ever done. My shoulder and arm ached badly, and I felt so sick that I nearly fell several times. But I managed it somehow. By using stones that stuck out from the wall more than the others, I got to the top. There was a low wall round the roof, and I lay down behind it, out of sight.

I must have been unconscious for some time, for I woke to hear the noise of a motor car engine and men's voices. Through a crack in the low wall I saw my three enemies come out of the house followed by a servant with a bandage round his head. They searched the garden and saw my footprints, but I had taken care to leave none near the dovecot, and after a time they gave up the search and returned to the house, blaming the unfortunate servant angrily.

All the hot afternoon I lay on the roof of the dovecot. I saw two men go off in the car, and another on a horse towards the moor. They were looking for me, and I wished them joy. Not far away I could see a stream flowing from the moor. I would have given a thousand pounds to put my face and head into it. But I saw something else, more interesting. Beyond the trees was an open space of grass, with a belt of trees all round. From the ground it looked like a wood, and no one would think there was an empty piece of grassland inside.

I didn't take long to guess what it was. It was a secret landing place for the aeroplane. This made me think of what would happen if it returned from one of its journeys – probably examining our coast and harbours – and the observer should see me. So I prayed for the coming of darkness, and glad I was when at last the sun went down over the western hills, and slowly the moor grew darker and darker.

The aeroplane was late. It was almost night when I saw it going down to its home in the wood. Lights moved about, and there was much coming and going from the house. Then darkness fell, and silence.

Thank God it was a black night. The moon would not rise till late. My thirst was too great to allow me to stay any longer, so about nine o'clock, as far as I could judge, I started to climb down. It wasn't easy, and half-way down I heard the door of the house open, and saw the light of a lamp moving. I hung where I was in terrible anxiety and pain for some minutes. Then the light disappeared, and I dropped as softly as I could to the ground.

I crept on my stomach till I reached the trees round the

house. If I had known how to do it I would have tried to put that aeroplane out of action, but I realised that any attempt would be useless. I was certain there would be some kind of defence round the house, so I went through the trees on hands and knees, feeling carefully every inch before me. It was a good thing, for soon I came on a wire about two feet from the ground. If I had fallen over that, it would doubtless have rung some bell in the house and I would have been taken prisoner. A hundred yards further on I found another wire cleverly placed beside the stream I had seen from the dovecot roof. Beyond that was the moor. I went on up the hill till I came to the other side and found another stream where I put my face in the cool refreshing water.

After that I did not stop till I had put half a dozen miles between me and that terrible house.

7. The meeting with the fisherman

I sat down on a hilltop to examine my position. I wasn't feeling very happy, for my natural thankfulness at my escape was clouded by my severe pain and discomfort of body. The smoke from that explosive had poisoned me, and the baking hot hours on the dovecot roof hadn't helped matters. I had a crushing headache and felt very sick. My shoulder was also in a bad way, and I could not use my left arm.

My plan was to find Turnbull's cottage, get my clothes and especially Scudder's notebook, and then reach the main railway line and go south. It seemed to me that the sooner I got in touch with the Foreign Office man, Sir Walter Bullivant, the better. I didn't see how I could get more proofs than I had already. He must just believe or disbelieve my story, and anyhow with him I would be in better hands than with the Black Stone. I had begun to feel quite friendly to the British police.

I got up and made my way with difficulty across the moors and hills to Turnbull's cottage. The cold wet weather made me ill, and I was in a miserable state when I knocked at the door.

Mr Turnbull himself opened to me. He was neatly dressed and shaved, and at first did not recognise me.

'Who are you to come knocking on a Sunday morning?' he asked.

I had lost all count of days. That explained his dress; he was going to church. My head was aching so badly that I could not answer. Then he recognised me and saw that I was ill.

'Have you got my glasses?' he asked.

I took them out of my pocket – luckily unbroken – and gave them to him.

'I suppose you've come for your coat,' he said. 'Come in. I say, you are too weak to walk! Let me help you to a chair.'

I could feel the fever coming on after the wet night, while my shoulder and the effects of the explosive combined to make me feel very bad. Mr Turnbull helped me off with my clothes, and put me to bed.

He was a true friend in need, the old roadman. Since his daughter's marriage he lived alone, for his wife had died years ago. For nearly ten days he did all the simple nursing I needed. It took five days for the fever to go, but I was very weak and unable to walk. He went out each morning, leaving me milk for the day, and locking the door behind him. In the evening he came in to sit with me. No one came near the place. He did not ask any questions, but brought me a paper sometimes. I saw that the interest in the Portland Place murder had died down.

One day he produced my belt from a locked drawer.

'There's a terrible lot of money in it,' he said. 'You'd better count it to see if it's all there.'

He never even asked my name. I wanted to know if anyone had been round making inquiries after my day of road-making.

'Yes,' he said, 'there was a man in a motor car. He asked who had taken my place that day. I pretended I thought him mad. But he kept on, so I said perhaps he meant my brother, who sometimes came to help me.'

As I got better I became very restless, and as soon as I felt strong enough, I decided to go. That was not till June 12th, when by good luck a friend of Turnbull's was going with some cows to Moffat, a town near the main railway line, and he offered to take me with him.

I made Turnbull accept five pounds for my lodging, but he was very unwilling to take it. He said he was only repaying my kindness to him, and he would hardly even say goodbye when I left.

I reached Moffat without accident or adventure and took the express train to the south. Next evening about eight o'clock I got to the village of Artinswell in the south of England.

I walked from the station up a road through a wood. After Scotland the air smelt heavy but sweet, for all round there were flowers on the trees. Soon I came to a bridge over a clear slow stream, and the quiet peace of the place put me at my ease. I began whistling as I looked into the stream, and the tune that came to my lips was 'Annie Laurie'.

A fisherman came up from the waterside, and as he neared me he, too, began to whistle. It was the same tune. He was a big man with a clever and good-tempered face. He leaned over the bridge with me.

'Clear water, isn't it?' he said pleasantly. 'Look at that big fish, four pounds in weight at least, but they are difficult to catch.'

'I don't see it,' said I.

'Look! There! A yard from the bank.'

'I see it now. It looks just like a black stone.'

'So,' he said, and whistled some more of 'Annie Laurie'.

'Twisdon's the name, isn't it?' he asked over his shoulder, his eyes still fixed on the stream.

'No,' I said. 'I mean to say, yes.' I had forgotten all about the name I had adopted.

'That's my house,' he said, pointing to a white gate a hundred yards up the road. 'Wait five minutes and then go round to the back door.'

I did as he told me. I found a pretty cottage with a garden beside the stream. It was full of the scent of flowers. The back door stood open, and a serious-looking butler was waiting for me.

'Come this way, sir,' he said, and led me along a passage and up some stairs to a pleasant bedroom looking towards the stream. There I found a complete set of clothes laid out for me, as well as shaving things and hair brushes.

'Sir Walter thought his nephew's clothes would fit you, sir. He always keeps some here, as he comes here every weekend. The bathroom is next door, sir, and I've prepared a hot bath. Dinner is in half an hour, sir. You'll hear the bell.'

It was like heaven to come suddenly from the life of a hunted beggar into this comfort. Clearly Sir Walter believed in me, though why he did I could not guess. I looked at myself in the glass and saw a wild, ill-looking, brown fellow, with a two-weeks' beard, dust in ears and eyes, collarless, with shapeless old clothes and boots that had not been cleaned for a month.

I did not waste time thinking how this sudden change had come, but I got into the bath, shaved and dressed. By the time I had finished, the looking-glass showed quite a neat young man.

Sir Walter was waiting for me in the dining room. The sight of him, so respectable, a high government official, the representative of law and order – gave me an unpleasant feeling that I was there under false pretences. He couldn't know the truth about me, or he wouldn't treat me like this. I could not go on without explaining.

'I'm more thankful to you, sir, than I can say,' I said, 'but I must make things clear. I'm wanted by the police, but I am guiltless of any crime. I have to tell you this, and I won't be surprised if you kick me out.'

41

He smiled. 'That's all right. Don't let that interfere with your enjoyment of dinner. We can talk about these things afterwards.'

And I did enjoy it. I laughed to think that I had been living for three weeks like a mountain robber, with every man's hand against me, and here I was being waited on by a butler in the house of Sir Walter Bullivant. After dinner we went to the smoking room for coffee. My host then told me to tell my story.

'I've done what Harry told me,' he said, 'and he promised I should hear something from you, Mr Hannay, that would wake me up.'

I began at the very beginning. I told him of my life in London, and the night I came back to find Scudder on my doorstep. He smiled to hear of the things Scudder told me, but became solemn when I spoke of the murder. I told him all about the milkman and my time in Galloway, and how I had read Scudder's cipher.

'You've got his notebook?' he asked sharply, and drew a long breath when I pulled it from my pocket.

I said nothing of what it contained. I described my meeting with Sir Harry, and he laughed aloud at my account of the political meeting. My day as a roadman excited him a bit. He made me describe the two fellows in the car very carefully, and the same with the old man at the moorland house.

'So you blew up his house, eh? Brave bit of work, that.'

Presently I came to the end of my wanderings. He got up slowly and looked down at me.

'You may dismiss the police from your mind,' he said. 'You're in no danger from the law of the land.'

'What!' I cried. 'Have they got the murderer?'

'No. But for the last two weeks they have taken you from their list of possible criminals.'

'Why?' I asked in astonishment.

'Chiefly because I received a letter from Scudder. I knew something of the man, and he often did work for me. He was a strange fellow, rather mad in some ways, but absolutely honest. The trouble with him was that he always wanted to do things alone. It made him useless as a secret agent of the government. I had a letter from him on May 31st.'

'But he had been dead a week by then.'

'The letter was written and posted on the 23rd. Clearly he did not think he was likely to die in the near future. His letters usually took a week to reach me, for they were sent under cover to Spain, and then to Newcastle. He loved to cover up his tracks, you know.'

'What did he say?'

'Nothing. Merely that he was in danger, but had found shelter with a good friend, and that I would hear from him before June 15th. He gave no address, but said he was living near Portland Place. I think his purpose was to clear you of suspicion if anything happened. When I got it, I went to Scotland Yard, examined the details of the inquiry into Scudder's death, and decided you were the friend. We made inquiries about you, Mr Hannay, and found you were respectable. I thought I knew the reasons for your disappearance – not only the police, but the other one too – and when I got Harry's letter I guessed at the rest. I have been expecting you any time this past week.'

You can imagine what a load this took off my mind. I felt a free man once more, for I was now against my country's enemies only, and not my country's law.

'Now let us have the little notebook,' said Sir Walter.

It took us an hour to work through it. I explained the cipher, and he was quick at understanding it. His face was very serious before he had finished, and he sat silent for a time.

'I don't know what to think of it,' he said at last. 'He is right about one thing – what is going to happen the day after tomorrow. How can it possibly have got known? That is serious enough in itself. But all this about war and the Black Stone – it sounds like some adventure story. I wish I had more confidence in Scudder's judgement. He wasn't satisfied with facts, but always imagined more than there really was in them.'

I remembered the story he had first told me – that was based on facts, but what a story!

'The Black Stone,' Sir Walter went on, '*Der Schwarzestein*. It's like a penny story book. And all this about Karolides. That is the weak part of it, for I happen to know that Karolides is likely to live longer than either of us. There is no government in Europe that wants him gone. No, Scudder has gone off the track there. Honestly, Hannay, I don't believe that part of the story.'

After a moment or two he continued: 'What is true is that there is some bad business going on, and he found out too much about it, and lost his life over it. Germany pays great attention to her secret agents' work, and gives high rewards to those who get important information, so they do not mind a murder or two to get it. They want our naval positions no doubt, but not for any special reason. They merely want their information to be complete.'

Just then the butler entered the room.

'There's a telephone call from London, Sir Walter. You are wanted personally.'

My host went off to the telephone. He returned in five minutes with a white face.

'I apologise to Scudder,' he said. 'Karolides was shot dead this evening a few minutes after seven.'

8. The coming of the Black Stone

I came down to breakfast next morning after eight hours of peaceful, dreamless sleep to find Sir Walter reading a cipher telegram from the government.

'I had a busy hour on the telephone after you went to bed,' he said. 'I got my chief to speak to the First Lord and the Secretary for War, and they are bringing General Royer over from France a day sooner. This telegram settles it. He will be in London at five.'

He asked me to help myself, and went on: 'Not that I think it will do much good. If your friends were clever enough to find out the first arrangement, they are clever enough to discover the change. I wish I knew how they get their information. We believed there were only five men in England who knew of Royer's visit, and less in France.'

While I ate, he continued to talk, taking me to my surprise into his confidence.

'Can't the naval arrangements be changed?' I asked.

'They could,' he said. 'But we want to avoid that if possible. They are the results of immense thought, and no change would be as good. Besides, on some points change is simply impossible. I suppose something might be done, if it was absolutely necessary. But you see the difficulty, Hannay. Our enemies are not going to be such fools as to rob Royer of his papers or any childish game like that. They know that would mean trouble, and put us on our guard. Their aim is to get the details without any one of us knowing, so that Royer will go back to Paris in the belief that the whole thing is still secret. If they can't do that, they fail, for, once we suspect, they know that the whole thing must be changed.'

'Then we must stay by the Frenchman's side till he is home again,' I said. 'If they thought they could get the information in Paris they would try there. It means that they have some deep plan in hand in London which they think will succeed.'

'Royer dines with my chief, and then comes to my house, where four people will see him – Whittaker from the Admiralty, myself, Sir Arthur Drew, and General Winstanley. The First Lord is ill, and perhaps will not be coming. At my house Royer will get an important paper from Whittaker, and after that he will be taken by motor car to Portsmouth, where a warship will take him to Havre in France. His journey is too important for the ordinary boat-train. He will never be left unguarded for a moment till he is safe in France. It will be the same with Whittaker till he meets Royer. That is the best we can do, and it's hard to see how

45

such arrangements can fail. But I don't mind confessing I'm afraid somehow. This murder of Karolides is going to cause trouble in Europe.'

After breakfast he asked me to take the place of Hudson, his car driver, and wear his clothes. I did so, and drove Sir Walter to London safely. It was a soft, breathless June morning, with a promise of heat later, and it was lovely going through the little towns and past the summer gardens of the Thames valley. We arrived at Sir Walter's house at half-past eleven. The butler was coming up by train with the bags.

The first thing he did was to take me round to Scotland Yard, and introduce me to Macgillivray, the Head of the Department.

'I've brought you the Portland Place murderer,' said Sir Walter.

The reply was a smile. 'It would have been a welcome present, Bullivant. This, I suppose, is Mr Hannay, who for some days greatly interested my department.'

'Mr Hannay will interest it again. He has much to tell you, but not today. For certain important reasons his story must wait for twenty-four hours. Then, I can promise you, you will be entertained. I want you to tell Mr Hannay that he will have no further trouble from the police.'

'Certainly, Mr Hannay. You can take up your life where you gave it up,' I was told. 'Your flat is waiting for you, and your man is still there.'

'We may want your help later on, Macgillivray,' Sir Walter said as we left.

Then he set me loose.

'Come and see me tomorrow, Hannay. I needn't tell you to keep deadly quiet. If I were you, I would go to bed, after so many days without proper sleep. You had better lie low, for if one of your Black Stone friends saw you there might be trouble.'

It was a strange feeling to have nothing to do. At first it was very pleasant to be a free man, able to go where I wanted without fearing anything. I had been only a month with the law against me, and it was quite enough for me. I went to a hotel and had a good lunch, but every time anyone looked at me, I wondered if they were thinking about the murder.

Then I took a taxi and drove miles away into North London. I walked back through fields and lines of streets, and it took me nearly two hours. All the time my restlessness was growing worse. I felt that great things were happening, or going to happen soon, and I, who was the centre of the whole business, was out of it. Royer would be landing at Dover, Sir Walter would be making plans with the few people in England who were in the secret, and somewhere underground the Black Stone would be working. I felt the shadow of danger coming near, and I had the curious feeling that I alone could prevent it. But I was out of the game now. How could it be otherwise? It was not likely that government ministers and Admiralty Lords and important army officers would admit me to their councils.

I actually began to wish I could run into one of my three enemies. That would lead to developments. I felt that I wanted a good fight in which I could hit somebody hard. I was rapidly getting into a bad temper.

I went to a restaurant for my evening meal, but didn't eat anything. I was no longer hungry. I was still restless. It seemed as if a voice kept speaking in my ear, telling me to keep moving, or the Black Stone would succeed. I felt sure that without me they would do so.

The result was that about half-past nine I made up my mind to go to Sir Walter's house. On the way I passed a group of young men in evening dress, probably going to a theatre. One of them was Jopley. He saw me and stopped suddenly.

'The murderer!' he cried. 'Here, you fellows, hold him! That's Hannay, the man who did the Portland Place murder!' He seized hold of my arm, and the others crowded round.

I wasn't looking for trouble, but my bad temper made me play the fool. A policeman came up, and I should have told him the truth, and if he didn't believe it, I could have demanded to be taken to Scotland Yard. But a delay at that moment seemed unbearable, and the sight of Jopley's stupid

47

face was more than I could stand. I struck out at him, and had the satisfaction of seeing him fall flat on the ground.

Then began a fearful fight. They were all on me at once, and the policeman came at me from behind. I got in one or two good blows, for I think in a fair fight I could have beaten the lot of them, but the policeman held me behind, and one of them got his fingers on my throat.

Through a black cloud of anger I heard the officer of the law asking what was the matter, and Jopley, between his broken teeth, declaring that I was Hannay the murderer.

I told the policeman that Scotland Yard knew all about me, and that he had better leave me alone, but it was no use.

'You've got to come along with me, young man,' he said. 'I saw you hit that gentleman first. He wasn't doing anything to you. You'd better come quietly, or I'll have to use force.'

Annoyance, and a feeling that nothing must delay me, gave me the strength of an elephant. I pulled the policeman off his feet, knocked down the man who had hold of my collar and set off as hard as I could go down the street. I heard a whistle being blown and the rush of men behind me.

I usually run at a good speed, and that night I had wings. In a moment I was round the corner and running towards St James's Park. There was a policeman at the gate, but I managed to trick him, and crossed the park safely.

Sir Walter's house was in a quiet street on the other side, and when I entered it, there was no one about. Outside the door were some motor cars waiting. I slowed to a walk as I reached the house. If the butler refused me admission, or even if he delayed in opening the door, I would be caught.

He didn't delay. The door opened as soon as I rang the bell.

'I must see Sir Walter,' I said breathlessly. 'My business is very important.'

That butler was a good fellow. He showed no surprise at all, but shut the door behind me.

'Sir Walter is busy, sir, and I have orders to admit no one. Perhaps you will wait.'

The house was an old-fashioned one, with a wide hall and

rooms on both sides of it. At the far end was a curtained corner with a telephone and a chair, which the butler offered me.

'See here,' I whispered. 'There's trouble about and I'm in it. But Sir Walter knows, and I'm working for him. If anyone comes and asks if I am here, tell him a lie.'

He bent his head respectfully, and next minute there was a noise of voices in the street, and a loud ringing of the bell. I never admired a man more than that butler. He opened the door, and with a calm face waited to be questioned. Then he told them quietly but firmly whose house it was, and what his orders were. They just melted from the doorstep. I saw it all from my corner, and it was as good as a play.

I hadn't waited long when there came another ring at the bell. The butler admitted this visitor at once. While he was taking off his overcoat, I saw who it was. You couldn't open a newspaper without seeing a photograph of that face, the neat grey beard, the firm mouth, the square nose, and the sharp blue eyes. I recognised the First Lord of the Admiralty, the man, they say, that made the British Navy what it was.

He passed my corner and was shown into a room at the back of the hall. I sat for twenty minutes, wondering what I was to do next. I looked at my watch. It was half-past ten, and in a quarter of an hour Royer would be leaving for Portsmouth.

Then I heard a bell ring, and the butler appeared. The door of the back room opened, and the First Lord came out. He walked past me, and in passing he looked in my direction, and for a second we looked each other in the face.

Only for a second, but it was enough to make my heart jump. I had never seen the great man before, nor he me. But in that moment of time something sprang into his eyes, and that something was recognition. You can't mistake it. It is a flash, a ray of light that suddenly goes out, but it means one thing and one only. It came unwillingly, for in a moment it died, and he passed on. In a confusion of wild fancies, I heard the street door close behind him.

I picked up the telephone book and found the number of his house. A servant answered my call.

'Is his Lordship at home?' I asked.

'His Lordship returned half an hour ago,' said the voice, 'and has gone to bed. He is not very well tonight. Will you leave a message, sir?'

I put the telephone receiver down, and fell back into the chair. My part in this business was not yet ended. And I had only just been in time.

Not a moment could be lost, so I marched without hesitation to the door of the back room, and entered without knocking. Five surprised faces looked up from a round table. There was Sir Walter, and Drew the War Minister, whom I knew from his photographs. There was a thin man, probably Whittaker, the Admiralty official, and General Winstanley. Lastly, there was a short, rather fat man who had stopped speaking as I came in.

Sir Walter's face showed surprise and annoyance.

'This is Mr Hannay, of whom I have spoken to you,' he said to the company. 'This is not a very suitable time for a visit, Hannay.'

I was feeling quite cool by now. 'We shall see,' I said, 'but I think I may be in time. Who was that who went out a minute ago?'

'Lord Alloa,' said Sir Walter, his face red with anger.

'It was not,' I cried. 'It was just like him, but it was not Lord Alloa. It was someone who recognised me, someone I have seen in the last month. As he left the doorstep, I telephoned to Lord Alloa's house and was told he had come in half an hour before and had gone to bed.'

'Then – who – who—' someone began.

'The Black Stone,' I cried, and sat down in the chair where 'Lord Alloa' had been sitting and looked round at five frightened faces.

9. The thirty-nine steps

'Nonsense!' said the official from the Admiralty.

Sir Walter got up and left the room while we sat in silence. He came back in ten minutes with a solemn face.

'I have spoken to Alloa,' he said. 'I got him out of bed – very annoyed. He was out to dinner tonight and went straight home.'

'But it's madness,' broke in General Winstanley. 'Do you mean to tell me that that man came here and sat beside me for nearly half an hour and that I didn't discover he was someone else?'

'Don't you see the cleverness of it?' I said. 'You were too interested in other things to have any eyes. You expected Lord Alloa. If it had been anybody else, you might have looked more closely, but it was natural for him to be here, and that put you all to sleep.'

Then the Frenchman spoke, slowly and in good English.

'The young man is right. He understands the working of the mind. Our enemies have not been foolish.'

He then told us of an adventure in West Africa. While fishing once, he left his little grey-brown horse tied to a tree. After an hour or so, he got up and went to the horse to get some food from a bag on its back. He put his hand up for the bag – and found it was a lion! The horse had been killed, and the man-eating lion had waited for him, standing in the horse's place.

'Consider, gentlemen,' he said. 'If I could make such a mistake in a land where a man is always on the watch for danger, why should we here in a peaceful town not make the same sort of mistake?'

'But I don't see,' said General Winstanley. 'Their plan was to get this information without our knowing it. It was only necessary for one of us to mention our meeting tonight to Lord Alloa for the deceit to be known.'

Sir Walter laughed. 'The choice of Alloa shows their cleverness. Which of us was likely to speak to him about tonight? Or was he likely to say anything about the subject?'

I remembered the First Lord's reputation for silence and quick temper.

'The thing that puzzles me,' said the General, 'is what good his visit here would do to that fellow? He could not carry away several pages of figures and strange names in his head.'

'That is not difficult,' the Frenchman replied. 'A secret agent has to have a good memory. He is trained for it. You noticed nothing, but he went through these papers again and again. I think it is safe to say he has every detail stamped on his mind. When I was younger I could do the same thing myself.'

'Well, I suppose there is nothing to do but change the plans,' said Sir Walter sadly.

Whittaker was looking very solemn. 'Did you tell Lord Alloa what has happened?' he asked. 'No? Well, I can't speak with absolute certainty, but I don't think we can change the arrangements to any extent unless we change the map of England.'

'Another thing must be said.' It was Royer who spoke. 'I talked freely when that man was here. I told something of the army plans of my government. I was permitted to say so much. But that information would be worth many millions to our enemies. No, my friends, I see no other way. The man who came here, and his companions, must be taken, and taken at once.'

'But we haven't the slightest idea where they are,' I cried.

'Besides,' said Whittaker, 'there is the post. By this time the news will be on its way.'

'No,' said the Frenchman. 'You do not understand the habits of a secret agent. He receives personally his reward, and he delivers personally his information. We in France know something of them. There is still a chance, my friends. These men must cross the sea, and there are ships to be searched and harbours to be watched. Believe me, the need is urgent, both for France and for Britain.'

Royer's calm good sense brought our minds back. He was the man of action among talkers. But I saw no hope in any face, and I felt none. Where among the fifty million of these islands and in less than a dozen hours were we to lay hands on the three cleverest criminals in Europe?

Then a sudden idea flashed into my mind.

'Where is Scudder's book?' I cried to Sir Walter. 'Quick, I remember something in it.'

He unlocked a drawer and gave it to me.

I found the place. 'Thirty-nine steps,' I read, and again, 'Thirty-nine steps, I counted them. High tide 10.17 p.m.'

The Admiralty man was looking at me as if he thought I had gone mad.

'Don't you see it's the key to the matter?' I shouted. 'Scudder knew where these fellows had their secret hiding place – he knew where they were going to leave the country, though he kept the name to himself. Tomorrow was the day, and it was some place where high tide was at 10.17.'

'They may have gone tonight,' someone said.

'Not they. They have their own secret arrangements made, and they won't be hurried. I know Germans and they are mad about keeping to a plan. Where can I get a book of tide tables?'

Whittaker became a bit more cheerful. 'It's a chance,' he said. 'Let us go over to the Admiralty.'

We got into two of the waiting motor cars – all but Sir Walter, who went off to find Macgillivray to get his help.

A search of the tide tables proved useless. There were at least fifty places where high tide was at 10.17. Then I thought of the steamships crossing to France and Belgium. But on looking through the list I found there were none at that time. Besides, high tide seemed important, so it might be a small harbour. But what about the steps? There were no sets of that many steps in any harbour I had ever seen. So I decided it must be a piece of open coast, and most likely on the east coast as that was nearest to Germany.

It struck me as strange that I should be sitting at a desk in the Admiralty with a government minister, an English and a French general, and other high government officials watching me, while from the notes of a dead man I was trying to drag a secret which meant life or death for us all.

Sir Walter joined us, and then Macgillivray. The latter had sent orders to the ports and railway stations for the three men I had described. Not that he or anyone else thought that this would do much good.

'Here's the most I can think out,' I said. 'We must find a place where there are several sets of stairs down to the shore, one of which has thirty-nine steps. I think it's a piece of open coast with fairly high cliffs, somewhere on the east coast. High tide there is at 10.17 tomorrow night.'

Then an idea struck me. 'Is there no chief of coastguards or some fellow like that who knows the east coast?'

Whittaker said there was, and that he would go and fetch him. We waited, doing nothing, till one in the morning when he came. He was a fine old fellow, with the look of a naval officer; he was very respectful to the company.

I left the War Minister to question him.

'We want you to tell us the places you know on the east coast where there are cliffs, and where several sets of stairs run down to the shore.'

He thought for a bit, and suggested various places where there were steps, but none of them appeared to be what we wanted.

'I can't think of anywhere else,' he said, 'except the Ruff.'

'What's that?' I asked.

'A big chalk cliff near Bradgate. It's got a lot of private houses on top, and some of them have steps down to the sands. It's a very high-class sort of place and the people there keep to themselves.'

I looked at the tide-table. High tide at Bradgate would be 10.27 on June 15th.

'We're on the track at last!' I cried excitedly. 'Do you know what the tide is at the Ruff?'

'Yes, sir. It's ten minutes before Bradgate.'

I closed the book and looked round at the company.

'If one of those sets of stairs has thirty-nine steps, we have solved the mystery, gentlemen,' I said. 'Sir Walter, I want you to lend me your car and a map of the roads. If Macgillivray will spare me ten minutes, I think we can prepare something for tomorrow.'

It seemed strange that I should take charge of the business like this, but they didn't seem to mind. I had been in it from the beginning, and I was used to rough work. It was General Royer who gave me permission.

'I for one,' he said, 'am content to leave the matter in Mr Hannay's hands.'

By half-past three I was driving rapidly through the moonlight towards the south-east coast, with Macgillivray's best man on the seat beside me.

10. To the sea coast

A beautiful June morning – it was the 15th at last – found me at Bradgate looking from my hotel window over the smooth sea. Two miles to the south a small warship was lying motionless. I found out her name and that of her commander from Scaife, Macgillivray's man, who had been a sailor himself, so I sent off a telegram to Sir Walter.

After breakfast Scaife went along to examine the houses on the Ruff. I walked with him along the sands, and sat down in a sheltered corner of the cliffs, as I didn't want to be seen, although there was no one on the shore at that hour.

It took him more than an hour to get the information we wanted without attracting anyone's attention, and as he came towards me looking at a bit of paper in his hand, I can tell you my heart was in my mouth. Everything depended, you see, on my guess proving right.

He read aloud the number of steps in the different stairs, 'Thirty-four, thirty-five, thirty-nine, forty-two, forty-seven,' and 'twenty-one' where the cliff was lower. I almost got up and shouted.

We hurried back to the town and sent a telegram to Macgillivray. I wanted half a dozen men. Then Scaife went back to have a look at the house at the head of the thirty-nine steps.

He came back with news that was rather puzzling. The house was called Trafalgar Lodge, and belonged to an old gentleman called Appleton, a retired business man. He was there a good deal in the summer, and was there now. He had been there for a week. There was nothing suspicious about the maids. Scaife went to the back door of the house pretending that he was an agent for sewing machines, and spoke to them. He was sure they knew nothing.

I borrowed Scaife's field-glasses, and before lunch took a walk along the Ruff. I kept well out of sight of the single row of houses, and found a good observation post on a piece of high ground behind. I could see Trafalgar Lodge very plainly with its garden on the sea side, and the steep stairs down the cliff.

I saw someone leave the house and walk along the cliff. It was an old man, wearing the usual summer dress of Englishmen on holiday by the sea. He was reading a newspaper, but sometimes looked through some glasses to the sea. He looked for a long time at the warship. When he returned to the house for lunch, I went back to Bradgate for mine.

I wasn't feeling very confident. This ordinary, honest-looking house was not what I had expected. The old man might be the old man of the house on the moor, or he might not. He was exactly the kind of satisfied old fellow you will find in every town and every holiday place. You could hardly find a more harmless sort of person anywhere.

But before lunch, as I was looking out to sea from the hotel door, I saw the thing I had hoped for, and been afraid to miss. A steam yacht came up from the south, and stopped almost opposite the Ruff. So Scaife and I went down to the harbour and hired a boat for an afternoon's fishing.

I spent a warm and peaceful afternoon fishing. We caught between us about twenty pounds of fish, and out in that dancing blue sea I took a more cheerful view of things. Above the white cliffs of the Ruff I saw the row of houses, and especially Trafalgar Lodge. About four o'clock, when we had fished enough, I made the boatman row us round the yacht, which lay like a delicate white bird, ready at a moment to fly. Scaife said she must be a fast boat, and had powerful engines.

Her name was the *Ariadne*, and I spoke to one of the sailors who was polishing some brass. He answered me in the voice of an English countryman. Another man spoke to us, and he, too, was unmistakably English. Then the men suddenly paid no attention to us, and went on with their work as an officer came along. He was a pleasant, clean-looking young fellow, and he put a question to us about our fishing in very good English. But there could be no doubt about him. His closely cut short hair and the kind of collar and tie he wore never came out of England.

That did something to give me confidence, but as we rowed back to Bradgate my doubts would not be dismissed. The thing that worried me was the thought that my enemies knew that I had got my knowledge from Scudder, and it was Scudder's notebook that had brought me to this place. If they knew Scudder knew this, would they not be certain to change their plans? The whole question was how much they understood about Scudder's knowledge. I wondered if the man last night had seen that I recognised him. Somehow I did not think he had, and I trusted to that.

In the hotel I met the commander of the warship and I had a few words with him. Then I went off to watch Trafalgar Lodge again. Two men were playing tennis in the garden. One was the old man I had already seen, the other a younger fellow. They played hard, like city gentlemen who wanted exercise. They shouted and laughed and stopped for drinks, which a maid brought out to them. I rubbed my eyes and asked myself if I was not the biggest fool in the world.

Mystery and darkness had hung about the men who hunted me over the Scottish moor in aeroplane and motor car, and especially about their old chief in that moorland house. It was easy enough to think of them as the killers of Scudder. But here were two harmless citizens doing what thousands of others like them were doing all over the country. Was I setting a trap to catch wild beasts, only to see two chickens in it?

A third man arrived, and was welcomed with more shouts and laughter, and English talk. They all went into the house, leaving me feeling a terrible fool. These men might be acting, but if so, where was their audience? They didn't know I was hiding behind some bushes thirty yards away.

And yet there were three of them; one was old, another fat, and the third was dark and thin. Their house agreed with Scudder's notes, and half a mile away lay a steam yacht with at least one German officer. I thought of Karolides lying dead, and all Europe trembling on the edge of war, and the men I had left behind in London anxiously waiting for the events of the next few hours.

I had to go on.

Then suddenly I remembered the fellow in South Africa whose advice had so helped me as a roadman. He had said that if a man could get into quite different surroundings from those in which he had been first observed, and – this is the important part – really behave in these surroundings as if he had never been out of them, he would puzzle the cleverest police in the world. A fool tries to look different; a clever man looks the same, and is different. He doesn't play a part; he lives a different life. That would explain the game of tennis, and their behaviour in the garden.

It was now nearly eight o'clock, and I went back and saw Scaife to give him his orders. I arranged with him how to place his men, and went for a walk till he was ready. At last, feeling more of a fool than ever, I went up to the door of Trafalgar Lodge and rang the bell.

I asked for Mr Appleton and followed the maid in. My plan had been to walk straight into the dining room, and by a sudden appearance wake in the men that sign of recognition that would prove I was right. But when I found myself inside the house, it seemed to master me. Tennis things, coats and hats, pictures on the wall, everything was exactly like what you would expect to see in ten thousand British homes of the middle class. The result was that when the maid asked my name, I gave it without thinking and let her go into the dining room. I had missed my chance of seeing them as they heard it, but I had the sense to follow her in at once.

When I walked into the room the old man at the head of the table had risen and turned to meet me. He was in evening dress – a short black coat and black tie, as was the other whom I called the fat one. The third, the dark fellow, wore a blue suit and a soft white collar.

The old man's manner was perfect. 'Mr Hannay?' he said hesitatingly. 'Did you wish to see me? One moment, you fellows, and I'll be back. We had better go to the smoking room.'

Though I hadn't any confidence left, I still had a little common sense. I pulled up a chair and sat down on it.

'I think we have met before,' I said, 'and I guess you know my business.'

The light in the room was not good, but so far as I could see, they played the part of being puzzled very well.

'Maybe, maybe,' said the old man. 'I haven't a very good memory, I'm sorry to say. You'll have to tell me your business, sir, for I really don't know it.'

'Well, then,' I said, and I didn't know whether I was talking foolishness or not, 'I have come to tell you that the game is up. I have here an order for the arrest of you three gentlemen.'

'Arrest!' said the old man, and he looked really shocked. 'Arrest? Whatever for?'

'For the murder of Franklin Scudder in London on the 23rd of last month.'

'I never heard the name before,' said the old man in a voice of astonishment.

One of the others spoke up. 'That was the Portland Place

murder. I read about it. But you must be mad, sir! Where do you come from?'

'Scotland Yard,' I said.

After that for a minute there was complete silence. The old man was a model of harmless frightened surprise. Then the fat one spoke.

'Don't worry, uncle,' he said. 'It is all a mistake; but these things happen sometimes, and we can easily set it right. It won't be hard to prove we had nothing to do with the murder. I can show I was not in England at that time, and Bob here was in hospital. You were in London, but you can explain what you were doing.'

'Right, Percy! Of course that's easy enough. It was the day after Agatha's marriage. Let me think. What was I doing? I came up to London after the party and had lunch at the Club with Charlie. Then – oh yes, I dined with Mr Fisher. I remember quite well, for I ate something or other not good for me, and was ill next day.'

'I think, sir,' said the young man politely to me, 'you will see you are mistaken. We want to help the law like all Englishmen, and we don't want Scotland Yard to be making fools of themselves. That's so, uncle?'

'Certainly, Bob.' The old man seemed to be getting his voice back. 'Certainly we'll do anything in our power to assist the authorities. But – but this is a bit too much.'

It couldn't be acting, it was all so natural. I almost felt like apologising and leaving them. As I have said, the light was not good, for there was only a lamp on the dining table. I got up and turned on the full room lights, and then looked carefully at the three faces.

Well, I didn't understand it at all. One was old, one fat, one dark and thin. They might easily be the three I had met in Scotland, but they might not. I can't explain why I, who have a good memory and strong powers of observation, could not find satisfaction.

'Well,' said the old man politely, 'are you satisfied, sir?'

I couldn't find a word, and sat down again. For a moment or two there was silence. I was thinking fiercely. They saw they had got me puzzled, and that put them at their ease.

Then suddenly something woke me. The old man had leaned back in his chair, his fingers tapping his knees.

It was the movement I remembered when I had stood before him in the moorland house with his armed servants behind me.

A little thing, lasting only a second, and I might easily have missed seeing it. But I didn't, and in a flash the air seemed to clear. Some shadow lifted from my brain and I was looking at the three men with full and absolute recognition.

The clock in the room showed ten.

The three faces before me seemed to change. The young one was the murderer. Now I saw cruelty where before I had seen pleasantness. His knife was the one that had fastened Scudder to the floor.

The fat one must have been a wonderful actor. Probably he was Lord Alloa of the night before. Scudder had said he lisped, and I could well understand him being able to adopt any manner of speech.

But the old man was the best. He was all brain, cold and pitiless. Now that my eyes were opened, I wondered where I had seen any kindness in his face.

'I say, Bob,' said the old man, 'look at the time. You'll have to be going if you want to catch your train. Bob has to go to London,' he added, turning to me.

I smiled. 'He'll have to make the journey another time,' I said.

At last they realised that they had not yet won. The old man tried again.

'I'll be responsible for my nephew,' he said. 'And you can have his address in London.'

As I looked at him, his eyelids fell in that bird-like manner which fear had stamped on my memory.

I blew my whistle.

In a second the lights were out. A pair of stong arms held me round the waist, covering the pockets in which a man might carry a gun.

'*Schnell, Franz,*' cried a voice, '*das Boot, das Boot!*'

As it spoke I saw two of my men in the moonlit garden. The dark young man jumped through the window and was through the garden before anyone could stop him. I seized hold of the old fellow, and the room seemed to fill with figures. The fat one was soon caught, but my eyes were for Franz, running for the steps. One man followed him but he had no chance. The gate of the stairs locked behind Franz, and he disappeared out of sight down the steps.

All this time I was holding the old man by the throat. Suddenly he broke away from me and threw himself to the wall. There was a sound like the turning on of the lights, but no light came. Instead, far below the ground came a noise of thunder, and through the window I saw a cloud of smoke and dust rising where the stairs had been.

Then someone put on the light. The old man was looking at me with burning eyes.

'He is safe,' he cried. 'You cannot follow in time . . . He is gone . . . *Der Schwarzestein ist in der Siegeskrone.*'

For the first time I realised what a terrible difficulty I had been up against. This man was more than a mere secret agent. In his own way he was a patriot.

As the police took him away, I said my last word to him.

'I hope Franz will enjoy his success. I forgot to tell you that the *Ariadne* for the last hour has been in our hands.'

Seven weeks later, as all the world knows, we went to war. I joined the New Army at once, and because of my experience in South Africa, was made an officer. But I had done my best service, I think, before the war began.

Questions

1 Why was Hannay tired of life in London?
2 What did he decide to do, and why did he change his mind?
3 Give a brief account of Scudder's story.
4 Did Hannay believe it? Why?
5 What made Hannay go cold with fear?

1 Why was Hannay in a terribly difficult position?
2 Why did Hannay decide to take Scudder's place?
3 Who would be likely to be after Hannay, and why?
4 What made him think of going to Galloway?
5 How did he escape from the flat?

1 How did Hannay try to throw the police off his track?
2 Explain how the milkman had been 'cheap at the price'.
3 What part was played by the dog?
4 Show how the tastes of the innkeeper helped Hannay.
5 How did Hannay escape from the inn?

1 Give a short account of the facts in Scudder's notebook.
2 What were Germany's real intentions?
3 What did the Black Stone want, and why?
4 What resulted from Hannay seeing the aeroplane?
5 Show how the accident was a lucky one for Hannay both immediately and in the future.
6 Who was Sir Walter Bullivant?

CHAPTER 5

1 Why did the open moorland seem like prison walls to Hannay?
2 How was Turnbull's daughter helpful to Hannay without realising it?
3 What steps did Hannay take to play the part of the roadman perfectly?
4 Give a short account of the meeting between Hannay and the Black Stone.
5 How did Hannay get through the circle of men surrounding him?

CHAPTER 6

1 Was Hannay wise to let Jopley go as he did? What was the result?
2 Why did Hannay begin to think he could not escape from the police on the moor?
3 How did the old gentleman treat Hannay?
4 What do you know of Ned Ainslie?
5 What was the terrible risk Hannay took? Why did he take it?
6 Give a short account of Hannay's escape from the house as Karl told it to his master when he returned in the car.

CHAPTER 7

1 What do you learn of Turnbull's character from this chapter?
2 Why did Sir Walter welcome Hannay to his house?
3 Why did Sir Walter apologise?

CHAPTER 8

1 What arrangements were made to keep the important paper safe?
2 What did Sir Walter think was the chief difficulty in making the arrangements?

3 What curious feeling did Hannay get? Did it prove to be right?

4 How and why did Hannay go to Sir Walter's house?

5 What was it that made Hannay's heart jump?

6 How was Hannay's suspicion proved to be correct?

CHAPTER 9

1 How was it that the men at the meeting did not know that it was not Lord Alloa who was there?

2 Why was it necessary to catch the Black Stone at once?

3 What happened in the Admiralty?

4 How was the meaning of Scudder's words about the thirty-nine steps discovered?

CHAPTER 10

1 When Hannay had found the thirty-nine steps what arrangements did he make?

2 Why didn't Hannay feel confident?

3 What plans had the Black Stone made to get their information to Germany?

4 Why was Hannay puzzled in the dining room at Trafalgar Lodge?

5 What caused him to see things clearly again?

6 How was the information prevented from leaving England?

GENERAL QUESTIONS

1 'The secret of playing a part is to think yourself into it.' Show from the story how this is true.

2 What important mistakes were made by both Hannay and his enemies?

3 How far did Hannay succeed by luck, and how far by his own cleverness?

4 'Scudder wasn't satisfied with facts, but always imagined more than there really was in them.' Was this true? And how far was this side of Scudder's character responsible for Hannay's adventures?

5 Which of the various people who helped Hannay were the most useful, and why?

6 Various events in this story are perhaps rather difficult to believe. Which is the most difficult? Explain why.

7 Would you like the life of a secret agent? Why?

8 If you wanted to escape from a place without being recognised how would you do it?

Glossary

Admiralty the government department that deals with the navy. The First Lord of the Admiralty is the minister in charge of the navy.

Balkan of the countries of south-east Europe.

butler the chief manservant in a big house.

cipher a secret way of writing.

City, the the business district of London, inside the old walled city.

dovecot a home for doves (birds that are regarded as a sign of peace).

game 'The game is up' means 'your criminal secrets are known, so you cannot succeed'.

lisp to pronounce S like Th.

lordship 'His Lordship' is the formal way of speaking of a lord.

maid a woman servant.

mine a case of explosives, put in the sea to destroy ships.

moor wild hilly land, covered with a rough plant called heather.

Near East the lands round the east end of the Mediterranean sea.

overall a thin coat worn over other clothes to keep them clean.

porter the man who guards the entrance of a block of flats.

prime the Prime Minister is the head of the government.

shepherd one who looks after sheep.

submarine a warship that goes under water.

surveyor a local official in charge of road work, etc.

yacht a small private ship, for racing or for pleasure.

German expressions

Schnell, Franz, das Boot 'Quick, Franz, the boat!'

Der Schwarzestein ist in der Siegeskrone 'The Black Stone is victorious!'

LONGMAN SIMPLIFIED ENGLISH SERIES

Notes

Notes

Notes

Notes